NATIONAL GEOGRAPHIC

D0503552

Using Your Senses at School

Jalmin Sweeney-Blight

You can use your senses
at school.

3

What can you see at school?

a classroom

a gym

a library

5

What can you hear at school?

children singing

a teacher talking

a ball bouncing

7

What can you feel at school?

a smooth desk

a soft
teddy
bear

a heavy bag

What can you smell at school?

flowers

Today is Friday

It is sunny today

a marker

food

11

What can you taste at school?

Lunch!